KENTUCKY DERBY GLASSES

PRICE GUIDE

1999-2000 Edition

A comprehensive guide to collecting
Kentucky Derby mint julep and shot glasses.

The Blood-Horse

The Blood-Horse, Inc. • www.bloodhorse.com
www.thehorse.com • 800-582-5604

Copywright ® 1999 The Blood-Horse, Inc.
All rights reserved. No part of this book may be reproduced in any form by any means, including photocopying, audio recording, or any information storage or retrieval system, without the permission in writing from the copyright holder. Inquiries should be addressed to Publisher, The Blood-Horse, Inc., Box 4038, Lexington, KY 40544-4038.

ISBN 1-58150-020-3

Printed in the United States of America

First Edition: April 1999

1 2 3 4 5 6 7 8 9 10

Contents

Introduction 1

A Piece of a Dream 2

Tips for Collecting Derby Glasses 4

Mint Julep Recipe 6

Julep Glasses 8

Julep Variations 38

Cordials, Shots & Jiggers 41

Quick Reference Price List 57

List of Derby Winners 59

Acknowledgements .60

Introduction

A rare, dated 1940 Derby glass for $15 bucks?! You can't believe your eyes. It's Saturday morning, and you're at the local flea market. 'Doesn't this person know what this is worth?' you think to yourself. It looks to be in good condition. You snatch it up. Score!

Most collectors of Kentucky Derby mint julep glasses are not going to be so fortunate as to find such an exquisite bargain. In fact, with the proliferation of Derby glass collectors out there and increasingly savvy sellers, it has become harder for collectors to know if they are getting a good price. For beginning collectors, learning which glasses to look for and how much the glasses are worth can be overwhelming.

The purpose of *The Blood-Horse Kentucky Derby Glasses Price Guide* is to provide new collectors, as well as established collectors, with an average market price to go by when scouring flea markets, yard sales, or even the Internet for mint julep glasses. Photos of the official glasses are provided to help with identification, as well as tips on the many variations and "mistakes" that collectors seek. In addition, this price guide has the first comprehensive list of all the Derby shot glasses, which were begun in 1987.

Take time to look at the photos of the glasses. Determine which ones you want and what year you want to begin with, then happy hunting!

Judy L. Marchman
Editor

1940
Dated
Glass
$16,500

PRICE GUIDE   1

Pieces of a Dream

Twenty-three years ago, John and Brenda Clark attended the Derby and came home with a plastic cup commemorating the event. Seventeen years ago, Vic Regnaud's wife, Peggy, came back from an auction with a bushel basket full of Kentucky Derby glasses.

Now, they count themselves among the thousands of avid Kentucky Derby memorabilia collectors.

For each, the key is not that they brought home a souvenir; the key is that they kept it. Because, like most everything else, if you just hold on to it long enough, there's a chance it will become collectible. And, more importantly, what becomes collectible becomes valuable.

So it is with Derby memorabilia. Just within the last decade, prices have skyrocketed.

Though the Derby glasses are by far the most popular item, collectors are also actively buying, selling, and trading anything connected to the world's best known race, such as programs, admission and mutuel tickets, lapel pins, photographs, posters, and advertising items.

You name it, if Kentucky Derby is on it, people are collecting it. Or perhaps trying to collect it is a more accurate description. Because, with Derby glasses, at least, this is pure Economics 101. In other words, supply and demand rules. So, while the age of a glass is obviously important, interestingly, some of the most frenzied action is on the newer items.

Case in point: a new limited edition of 1,000 numbered glasses released for the 1997 race was quickly sold out and has already seen several of the $20 gold-plated tumblers sold for $150.

John Clark, who lives in Frankfort, Ky., divides the glass collectors into three groups of people: those who have glasses from 1974 to the present; those who then decide to go back a little further; and finally, those who become obsessed and try to secure all the glasses.

The problem is, there are very few "complete" collections because no one knows for sure how many of certain glasses exist. What is known is this: though a water glass dated 1938 is known to exist, many collectors accept the 1939 as the first. Why? Because the 1938 was used as a beverage glass in the Churchill Downs clubhouse while the 1939 was the first julep glass manufactured to sell.

"We really don't know how many of certain early years there are, because some people, if they have one, don't want anyone else to know," Clark said.

The rarest glass is the 1940, which had a total production of only 800. Though no one knows how many still exist, there are thought to be only a handful. Most experts agree its value is at least $10,000-plus.

One that does exist is kept in Clark's bank lockbox. His personal rule of thumb is any glass that becomes worth $1,000 or more moves from the wood and glass cabinet in his house to safekeeping at the bank.

Clark has owned the crown jewel of Derby glasses for several years, though he politely refuses to say how much he paid for it. "I was in Georgetown (Kentucky) at an antique mall and someone came up behind me and asked me if I wanted to buy a 1940 Derby glass," he recalled of the circumstances surrounding his acquisition of the glass. "I didn't have the money on me, but I went and cashed a check right then and bought it."

And how did the seller get the glass? Clark cringes when he tells this part of the story. "It was found for $5 in an antique shop in Owensboro." Just down the road.

Suffice it to say Clark paid considerably more than $5. But, he knows it is worth much more today. Plus, he is one of the few people to have a complete collection. "Someday I guess I'll sell it," he said of the 1940. "But the thing is, if you do that, you've broken up your collection."

Though most racing fans are familiar with the glass of today—the one in which mint juleps are served on Derby Day—Derby glasses have taken on many shapes, sizes, and textures in their 60-year history. The best known—and most valuable—of these "different" glasses were produced from 1941 to 1944. Because aluminum and glass were being rationed during World War II, bakelite plastic was used instead.

These speckled glasses, commonly called Beetleware after the company that manufactured them, exist in various colors, with blue, grey, and yellow considered the rarest. Most collectors agree there are at least nine different colors of

bakelite glasses, others known to exist including pink, orange, red, white, brown, and green.

Because many collectors feel no two bakelite glasses are exactly alike, they are among the most popular to collect. They are known to bring $2,500 to $7,000 in good condition, more than any glass other than the rare 1939s and 1940s. Vic Regnaud is especially enamored with the bakelite glasses.

"I have over 1,000 glasses, but the Beetleware are my favorites," said Regnaud, who is originally from England but now resides in Perry Park, Ky. He began collecting because his wife purchased some glasses at an auction and he was "intrigued" by them.

"She came home with a whole bushel basket full from the '40s," he said. "There was no collector interest then...people then didn't even know the difference between a Derby and bar glass."

When the first collector's price guide was published, Regnaud became more interested in the glasses. "I continued the set by purchasing glasses for my wife as birthday presents...now it's a passion."

Regnaud counts himself among those who are "very surprised" at how quickly prices are rising for glasses. "You take a glass that four or five years ago you could sell for $800, today it's worth $3,500. Right now there's just an intense amount

of collectors who all want the same glass."

With so many collectors in search of the same glasses, it is only natural that middle men—dealers —come in the picture. A member of that growing group is Joe Boone, who lives in Louisville, Ky. Boone has been dealing in Derby products since 1993 and has booths in four different antique malls, two in Louisville, and also in nearby Shepherdsville, Ky., and Seymour, Ind. Boone keeps a stock of all Derby glasses since 1945 and also has shot glasses, bar glasses, programs, and admission items.

"I've always enjoyed trading things, and I love horses, so this is a perfect business for me," Boone said.

Like Regnaud, Boone is another who talks about the rapid rise in prices associated with Derby items. "The first year they did the Derby shot glasses was 1987 and they did four," he said. "They made two jiggers, a red and gold and a black and gold, and two ounce and a half glasses, one frosted and one clear. In 1993, I could buy the red and gold jigger for $400. Now I have customers looking for it willing to pay $2,000."

Besides the antique malls, Boone regularly trades Derby items through the Internet and has his own Web site.

One of the more elaborate Web sites belongs to Cindy Pierson, a collector who lives in Montgomery, Ala. Pierson's site shows photographs of many of her racing collectibles.

Describing herself as "one of those girls who grew up loving horses," Pierson only first heard of Derby glasses three years ago. Now, she has 300 Derby glasses as well as other items such as programs, ticket stubs, and pins.

One of the largest Derby collections belongs to Kent Rea. With so many items accumulating, Rea built a 1,000-square-foot room just to house them. Actually, he doesn't call it a room, but his "museum." Rea has over 3,000 different glasses, but his bakelites are among his favorites. "They're so pretty, and I really believe that no two are exactly alike. There's just so much mystique about them." Rea, originally from Louisville, also collects programs, mutuel tickets, advertising pieces, and prints of the Triple Crown winners.

"Every auction I go to I pick up one or two things," said Rea. "Half the fun is looking...I've found things in little places for next to nothing. I guarantee you if you see a dealer price for something, you can find it somewhere for half that price."

And, if you do find it for half that price, hold on to it. It will be worth more before you can say "greatest two minutes in sports."

By Dan Liebman

(*reprinted from the 1997* Kentucky Derby Official Souvenir Magazine, *published by* The Blood-Horse)

Tips for Collecting Kentucky Derby Glasses

A few Derby glasses picked up here and there have turned into a new obsession: collect all the glasses. But how to get started? Tom Sporney, a Derby glass collector from Indianapolis, Ind., provided answers to some of the questions beginning collectors might ask. Sporney and his wife, Jane, have been collecting Derby glasses since about 1987.

What is the best strategy to take when starting a collection?

Conventional wisdom dictates that serious beginners should buy older glasses first, such as ones from the 1940s, '50s, and '60s. These are rarer and are increasing in value rapidly. Sporney offered some words of caution for beginners: purchase the older and less available glasses that you can afford within a somewhat flexible budget.

What does mint condition mean?

Mint condition indicates the glass is as close as possible to looking like it did straight from the factory, e.g., no scratches, chips, or fading.

What sort of things should I look for when examining glasses?

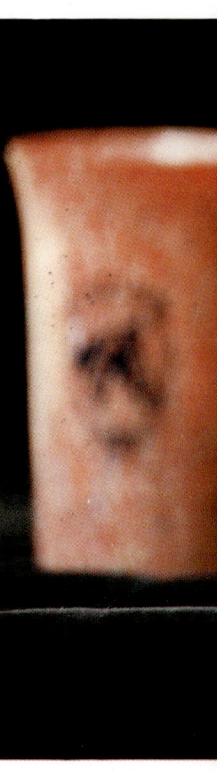

Characteristics of the glass

- Roundness: variations in roundness greater than 1/32" to 1/16" range are easily visible.
- Top edge: minor enlargement of drinking lip at finish point acceptable as production standard, noticeable bulbous protrusion at finish point not desirable.
- Bubbles within the glass: small incidental air bubble within glass acceptable as production standard. Multiple or large visible air bubbles not desirable.

Printing

- Completeness: no voids, uniformity of inking.
- Symmetry: centered indexing when different colors/screens are used.
- No Fading or "loss of gloss": dishwashing, sunlight, etc.

General

- No physical scratches or gouges, in printing or on the glass.
- Distinguish between a "production error" and a "handling flaw."

What is meant by "mistakes" and "variations"?

It is really just a matter of nomenclature, just to distinguish one non-standard item from the "normal" one, and also to distinguish between production and flaw.

What kind of places should I frequent to look for glasses?

Anywhere and everywhere, even the obvious places. "Our best finds have been in the 'nah, can't be anything here' locations," said Sporney. "Cindy (Pierson, a fellow collector from Alabama) and I split a set of four '74 Federals at the big monthly flea market in Atlanta when I walked over to unstack the dealer's display where he nested glasses."

Yard sales, flea markets, and off-the-road shops are still the best places to look for glasses, especially bargains.

What about the Internet?

A number of dealers and collectors have Web sites. A good index of these sites can be found at Cindy Pierson's Horse Racing Web Site Index at http://members.xoom.com/horseracing/. Just click on the "Collecting, Art, Photos" category. Or try the Haynet at http://www.haynet.net/.

Another popular site is eBay.com, which is an auction site for anything collectible. Racing has its own section, and Derby glasses abound, but Sporney cautions that finding bargains has become increasingly difficult on eBay. The site address is http://www.ebay.com/. Horse racing is located under the Sports Memorabilia category.

Other sites of note include The Equillector, a guide for collectors of horse racing memorabilia, at http://members.xoom.com/equillector/ and Joe Boone's The Derby Glass Page at http://derbyglass.com/.

Mint Julep

•

2 cups sugar
2 cups water
Crushed ice
Kentucky bourbon
Fresh mint

Boil sugar and water together for 5 minutes to make a syrup. Cool, place in covered container with 6 to 8 fresh mint sprigs. Refrigerate overnight.

Fill each julep glass with crushed ice, add 1 tablespoon of mint syrup and 2 ounces of Kentucky bourbon. Stir rapidly to frost outside of glass. Garnish with frest mint sprig. Enjoy!

(The Early Times recipe)

•

Kentucky Derby Glasses Price Guide

Julep Glasses

1 9 3 8

1938
$3,065

Some collectors do not consider this an "official" Derby glass. However, it is sought after as the starting point for many collections because it is dated and was used as a water glass at Churchill Downs on Derby Day.

1939
$6,030

1940

1940
Aluminum
$580

These tumblers, including the French Lick version, are rapidly escalating in value and are becoming difficult to find, especially in mint condition.

1940
Aluminum, French Lick
$1,000

This version was produced by the French Lick Springs Hotel in Indiana.

1940

1940

Glass, undated (shown), $13,000
Glass, dated (see page 1), $16,500

Both of these glasses are considered rare and are in great demand with collectors.

1941-1944

Beetleware
$2,500/up

(from left, red, blue-grey, mottled pink) Also known as Bakelites, these tumblers come in a variety of colors and shades. They were produced during World War II when glass and aluminum were rationed.

1945

Tall
$400

Short
$1,130

Jigger ("Juice")
$800

1948

Clear bottom
$190

Frosted bottom
$220

1949
$190
Variation with year/winner missing
$530

1950
$370

1951
$515

1952
$190
The "Gold Cup" Julep

KENTUCKY DERBY JULEP GLASSES

1953

1953
$130
This was the year past winners started to be listed on a regular basis.

1954
$190

14 THE BLOOD-HORSE

KENTUCKY DERBY JULEP GLASSES

1955

1955
$130

1956

2 stars, 3 tails
$190

2 stars, 2 tails
$185

1 star, 2 tails
$205

1 star, 3 tails
$460

PRICE GUIDE 15

1957

1957
$110

1958
Gold Bar (left)
$180
Iron Liege
$210

The Iron Liege version was produced from overstocked 1957 glasses, restamped with that year's winner.

1959
$65

1960
$70

Kentucky Derby Julep Glasses

1961

1961
$100

1962
$70

1963
$50

1964
$40

1965

1965
$70

1966
$50

1967
$50

1968
$50

1969

1969
$45

No past winners are listed because of the 1968 disqualification of Dancer's Image.

1970
$60

More valuable because the type of glass used breaks easily.

KENTUCKY DERBY JULEP GLASSES

1971

1971
$40

1972
$40

PRICE GUIDE 23

1973

1973
$50

White background
(see page 38)
$100

1974

Canonero "Federal"
$155

Canonero II
"Federal"
$160

Canonero "Libbey"
$12

Canonero II
"Libbey"
$13

This was the first year julep glasses were sold off-track. "Libbey" is Libbey Glass Co. and "Federal" is the Federal Glass Co.

1975
$10

1976

Glass
$14

Plastic tumbler
$20

The plastic tumbler was produced for the infield.

1977

1977
$8

1978
$10

1979
$10

1980
$20

"Green screened" horse, $1,275

"Dark brown screened," $150

Kentucky Derby Julep Glasses

1981

1981
$13

1982
$11
"Red dot" missing
(see page 39)
$500

1983
$9

1984
$8
"Red Dot" missing
(see page 39)
$500

1985
$10

1986
1985 copyright
$20
1986 copyright
$11
"The Tiffany Glass"

1987
$8

1988
$8

1
9
8
9

1989
$8

1990
$6

KENTUCKY DERBY JULEP GLASSES

1991
$6

1992
$6

PRICE GUIDE

1
9
9
3

1993
$6

1994
$5

1995
$5

1996
$5

1997

1997
$4

1998
$4

Kentucky Derby Julep Glasses

1999

1999
$3

Julep Variations

1946

1946-47

Leftover blanks from 1945. Some collectors do not consider these "official" glasses because they can be difficult to authenticate as actually being used at Churchill Downs.

No value available.

1973

(from left) A regular 1973 julep glass and a "white" background variation.

See page 24 for prices.

KENTUCKY DERBY JULEP VARIATIONS

1982

1982 and 1984

The "red dot" indicating a filly won the Derby was left off of Genuine Risk's name on some of the glasses in 1982 (left) and 1984.

See pages 28-29 for prices.

1990

Like 1973, this glass also has the white background variation (right).

No value available for white variation.

PRICE GUIDE 39

KENTUCKY DERBY JULEP VARIATIONS

1997

1997-1999

Ltd. Edition (1,000) 22k Gold Mint Julep Glass Series. Letters of authenticity are included.

1997 $150
1998 $80
1999 $80

Signature Series

Begun in 1992, a limited edition series with the year's glass signed by the winning jockey.

1992 $175
1993 $125
1994/on $50

Cordials, Shots & Jiggers

1987

3 oz. Jigger	Clear Glass—red/gold lettering $1,590
3 oz. Jigger	Clear—black/gold $515
1 1/2 oz. Shot	Clear—red/black/yellow $270
1 1/2 oz. Shot	Frosted—red/black/yellow $330

1988

3 oz. Jigger	Clear—Multi-Color $65
1 1/2 oz. Shot	Clear—Multi-Color $55
2 oz. Ceramic Shot	White—Multi-Color $150

KENTUCKY DERBY GLASSES/CORDIALS, SHOTS & JIGGERS

1989

1989

3 oz. Jigger	Clear—Multi-Color	$40
3 oz. Jigger	Clear—Struck Equipt. Co.	$250
1 1/2 oz. Shot	Clear—Multi-Color	$40

1990

3 oz. Jigger	Clear—Multi-Color	$250
1 1/2 oz. Shot	Clear—Multi-Color	$35

THE BLOOD-HORSE

1991

3 oz. Jigger	Clear—Multi-Color	$40
1 1/2 oz. Shot (Libbey)	Clear—Multi-Color	$35
1 1/2 oz. Shot (Korean)	Clear—Multi-Color	$55

1992

3 oz. Jigger	Clear—Multi-Color	$30
1 1/2 oz. Shot (Libbey)	Clear—Multi-Color	$40
1 1/2 oz. Shot (Korean)	Clear—Multi-Color	$20
1 1/2 oz. Shot	Black—Gold	$20

KENTUCKY DERBY GLASSES/CORDIALS, SHOTS & JIGGERS

1993

Cordial (handle) with back copy	Clear—Multi-Color	$85
Cordial (handle) without copy	Clear—Multi-Color	$50
Cordial with back copy	Clear—Multi-Color	$260
Cordial without copy	Clear—Multi-Color	$70
Cordial (handle) without copy	Clear—Gold	$500

Note: This was the first year Cordials were produced.

1993

1 1/2 oz. Shot (Libbey)	Clear—Multi-Color	$25
1 1/2 oz. Shot (Korean)	Clear—Multi-Color	$15
1 1/2 oz Shot	Black—Gold	$25
1 1/2 oz. Shot	Black—Multi-Color	$25
3 oz. Jigger	Clear—Multi-Color	$25
1 1/2 oz. Shot	Black—Gold/Solid Screen	$150

Kentucky Derby Glasses/Cordials, Shots & Jiggers

1994

Cordial without copy	Clear—Multi-Color	$20
Cordial with copy	Clear—Multi-Color	$20
Cordial (handle) w/o copy	Clear—Multi-Color	$20
Cordial (handle) w/copy	Clear—Multi-Color	$20

1994

3 1/2 oz. Boreal	Clear—Multi-Color	$140
3 oz. Jigger	Clear—Multi-Color	$15
1 1/2 oz. Shot	Black—Multi-Color	$15
1 1/2 oz. Shot	Clear—Multi-Color	$15

Note: This was the first year Boreals were made.

KENTUCKY DERBY GLASSES/CORDIALS, SHOTS & JIGGERS

1995

3 1/2 oz. Boreal	Clear—Multi-Color	$20
3 oz. Jigger	Clear—Multi-Color	$10
2 oz. Whiskey Shot	Clear—Black/Gold	$15
1 1/2 oz. Shot	Black—Black Twin Spires	$15
1 1/2 oz. Shot (Hunter)	Clear—Multi-Color	$10
1 1/2 oz. Shot	Black—White Twin Spires	$100
1 1/2 oz. Shot (Libbey)	Clear—Multi-Color	$20

1995

Cordial (handle) w/o copy	Clear—Multi-Color	$10
Cordial with copy	Clear—Multi-Color	$15
Cordial (handle) w/copy	Clear—Multi-Color	$10
Cordial without copy	Clear—Multi-Color	$15

1996

*Cordial (handle) w/o copy	Clear—Etched $70
*Cordial without copy	Clear—Etched $70
Cordial with copy	Clear—Multi-Color $15
Cordial (handle) w/copy	Clear—Multi-Color $10
Cordial (handle) w/o copy	Clear—Multi-Color $8
Cordial without copy	Clear—Multi-Color $10

1996

*3 oz. Boreal	Clear—Etched $100
3 oz. Boreal	Clear—Multi-Color $10

Note: A number of "unauthorized" shots were produced for 1996. Production quantities of these could range anywhere between 72 and 500. These glasses are indicated with an asterisk (*).

1996

*1 1/2 oz. Shot	Clear—Etched	$70
*2 oz. Square Shot	Clear—Etched	$100
*1 1/2 oz. Paneled Shot	Clear—Etched	$90

1996

*1 1/2 oz. Shot   Wine—Multi-Color ......Factory Sample
(no value available)

Kentucky Derby Glasses/Cordials, Shots & Jiggers

1996

1 1/2 oz. Shot	Clear—Multi-Color	$8
*2 oz. Square Shot	Clear—Multi-Color	$100
*1 1/2 oz. Paneled Shot	Clear—Multi-Color	$70
*2 oz. Flared Shooter	Clear—Multi-Color	$60
3 oz. Jigger	Clear—Multi-Color	$10

1996

1 1/2 oz. Shot	Green—Raised Decal (Came as part of set of 3 shots, including Black and Cobalt)	$15
*1 1/2 oz. Shot	Green—True Etched	$100
*1 1/2 oz. Shot	Green—Multi-Color	$85

Price Guide 49

1996

*1 1/2 oz. Shot	Black—Etched	.$70
1 1/2 oz. Shot	Black—Multi-Color	.$20
1 1/2 oz. Shot	Black—Gold (Came as part of a set of three shots, including Green and Cobalt)	.$10

1996

1 1/2 oz. Shot	Cobalt—Gold (Came as part of a set of three shots, including Green and Black)	.$10
*1 1/2 oz. Shot	Cobalt—Multi-Color	.$100
*1 1/2 oz. Shot	Cobalt—Etched	.$80

1996
*2 oz. Ceramic Shot   White—Multi-Color $75
2 oz. Whiskey Shot   Clear—Black/Gold $10

1997
2 oz. Cordial   Cobalt—Gold $9
1 1/2 oz. Shot   Clear—Black/Gold $8

KENTUCKY DERBY GLASSES/CORDIALS, SHOTS & JIGGERS

1997
1 1/2 oz. Shots   Wine, Cobalt, Green—Gold (sold as a set)
                                    . . . .$40 (for set)
1 1/2 oz. Shot   Black—Gold $7

1997
2 oz. Whiskey Shot   Clear—Gold $10
2 oz. Whiskey Shot   Clear—Etched (Bacon's/McAlpin's department
                               store limited edition) $50
3 oz. Jigger   Clear—Gold $8

Kentucky Derby Glasses/Cordials, Shots & Jiggers

1997

1 1/2 oz. Ceramic Shot	White—Graffiti	$10
1 1/2 oz. Square Shot	Clear—Multi-Color	$10
1 1/2 oz. Shot	Clear—Multi-Color	$7
Cordial without copy	Clear—Multi-Color	$10
1 1/2 oz. Ceramic Shot	White—Multi-Color	$8

1998

1 1/2 oz. Shots	Black, Green, Cobalt—Gold (sold as a set) .... $28 (for set)
1 1/2 oz. Shot	Black—Multi-Color $8

PRICE GUIDE

1998

Lg. Shooter with handle	Clear—Multi-Color	$12
Cordial w/o copy	Clear—Multi-Color	$9
2 oz. Whiskey Shot	Clear—Gold	$8
2 oz. Whiskey Shot	Clear—Etched (Bacon's/McAlpin's limited edition)	$30

1998

1 1/2 oz. Ceramic Shot	White—Multi-Color	$7
2 oz. Square Shot	Clear—Multi-Color	$7
3 oz. Jigger	Clear—Gold	$8
1 1/2 oz. Shot	Clear—Multi-Color	$7
1 1/2 oz. Shot	Clear—Gold (Ltd. Edition, 1/1000) (Part of Triple Crown set)	$30

1999
1 1/2 oz. Shots   Cobalt, Black, Green—Gold (sold as a set)
.... $18 (for set)

1999
1 1/2 oz. Shot	Clear—Multi-Color $5
2 oz. Flared Shooter	Clear—Multi-Color $6
Cordial w/o copy	Clear—Multi-Color $7
Cordial (handle) w/o copy	Clear—Multi-Color $7
2 oz. Whiskey Shot	Clear—Multi-Color $6

KENTUCKY DERBY GLASSES/CORDIALS, SHOTS & JIGGERS

1
9
9
9

1999
1 1/2 oz. Stainless Steel Shot (Ltd. Edition, 1/1000) $16

1999
1 1/2 oz. Shot   Clear—Checkerboard Wrap $7

Quick Reference Price List

To determine values for this price guide, several prominent collectors and/or dealers, primarily from but not exclusive to the Louisville, Ky., area, were polled as to what they would consider paying for the Kentucky Derby glasses. The numbers were averaged to produce the values given below, which are intended to represent a "fair market value." The same method was used for determining the values on the Kentucky Derby shot glasses. As with anything collectible, prices will fluctuate based on several factors, including buyer demand, location, and luck.

Kentucky Derby Mint Julep Glasses

Year	Value	Year	Value	Year	Value
1938	$3,065	1958 (Iron Liege)	210	1978	10
1939	6,030	1958 (Gold Bar)	180	1979	10
1940 (Undated, Glass)	13,000	1959	65	1980	20
1940 (Dated, Glass)	16,500	1960	70	1980 (Green Horse)	1,275
1940 (Aluminum)	580	1961	100	1980 (Dark Brown)	150
1940 (Aluminum, French Lick)	1,000	1962	70	1981	13
		1963	50	1982	11
1941-44 (Beetleware)	2,500/up	1964	40	1982 (red dot missing)	500
1945 (Tall)	400	1965	70	1983	9
1945 (Short)	1,130	1966	50	1984	8
1948 (clear bottom)	190	1967	50	1984 (red dot missing)	500
1948 (frosted bottom)	220	1968	50	1985	10
1949	190	1969	45	1986 (1985 copyright)	20
1949 (year/winning missing)	530	1970	60	1986 (1986 copyright)	11
1950	370	1971	40	1987	8
1951	515	1972	40	1988	8
1952	190	1973	50	1989	8
1953	130	1973 (white background)	100	1990	6
1954	190	1974 (Canonero "Federal")	155	1991	6
1955	130	1974 (Canonero II "Federal")	160	1992	6
1956 (2 stars, 3 tails)	190	1974 (Canonero "Libbey")	12	1993	6
1956 (2 stars, 2 tails)	185	1974 (Canonero II "Libbey")	13	1994	5
1956 (1 star, 2 tails)	205	1975	10	1995	5
1956 (1 star, 3 tails)	460	1976 (Glass)	14	1996	5
1957	110	1976 (Plastic tumbler)	20	1997	4
		1977	8	1998	4
				1999	3

Kentucky Derby Shot Glasses (H-handle)

Year	Style	Color—Lettering	Value	Year	Style	Color—Lettering	Value
1945				1989			
4 oz.	Jigger	Clear—Green Lettering	$800	1 1/2 oz.	Shot	Clear—Multi-Color	40
1987				3 oz.	Jigger	Clear—Multi-Color	40
1 1/2 oz.	Shot	Clear—Red/Black/Yellow	270	3 oz.	Jigger	Clear—Struck Equipt. Co.	250
1 1/2 oz.	Shot	Frosted—Red/Black/Yellow	330	1990			
3 oz.	Jigger	Clear—Red/Gold	1,590	1 1/2 oz.	Shot	Clear—Multi-Color	35
3 oz.	Jigger	Clear—Black/Gold	515	3 oz.	Jigger	Clear—Multi-Color	250
1988				1991			
1 1/2 oz.	Shot	Clear—Multi-Color	55	1 1/2 oz.	Shot (Libbey)	Clear—Multi-Color	35
3 oz.	Jigger	Clear—Multi-Color	65	1 1/2 oz.	Shot (Korean)	Clear—Multi-Color	55
2 oz.	Ceramic Shot	White—Multi-Color	150	3 oz.	Jigger	Clear—Multi-Color	40

Quick Reference Price List (continued)
Kentucky Derby Shot Glasses (H-handle)

Year	Style	Color—Lettering	Value
1992			
1 1/2 oz.	Shot (Libbey)	Clear—Multi-Color	40
1 1/2 oz.	Shot (Korean)	Clear—Multi-Color	20
1 1/2 oz.	Shot	Black—Gold	20
3 oz.	Jigger	Clear—Multi-Color	30
1993			
1 1/2 oz.	Shot (Libbey)	Clear—Multi-Color	25
1 1/2 oz.	Shot (Korean)	Clear—Multi-Color	15
1 1/2 oz.	Shot	Black—Gold	25
1 1/2 oz.	Shot	Black—Gold/Solid Screen	150
1 1/2 oz.	Shot	Black—Multi-Color	25
3 oz.	Jigger	Clear—Multi-Color	25
	Cordial with back copy	Clear—Multi-Color	260
	Cordial without copy	Clear—Multi-Color	70
	Cordial (H) w/copy	Clear—Multi-Color	85
	Cordial (H) w/o copy	Clear—Multi-Color	50
	Cordial (H) w/o copy	Clear—Gold	500
1994			
1 1/2 oz.	Shot	Clear—Multi-Color	15
1 1/2 oz.	Shot	Black—Multi-Color	15
3 oz.	Jigger	Clear—Multi-Color	15
	Cordial w/copy	Clear—Multi-Color	20
	Cordial w/o copy	Clear—Multi-Color	20
	Cordial (H) w/copy	Clear—Multi-Color	20
	Cordial (H) w/o copy	Clear—Multi-Color	20
3 1/2 oz.	Boreal	Clear—Multi-Color	140
1995			
1 1/2 oz.	Shot (Hunter)	Clear—Multi-Color	10
1 1/2 oz.	Shot (Libbey)	Clear—Multi-Color	20
1 1/2 oz.	Shot	Black—Black Twin Spires	15
1 1/2 oz.	Shot	Black—White Twin Spires	100
2 oz.	Whiskey Shot	Clear—Black/Gold	15
3 oz.	Jigger	Clear—Multi-Color	10
	Cordial w/copy	Clear—Multi-Color	15
	Cordial w/o copy	Clear—Multi-Color	15
	Cordial (H) w/copy	Clear—Multi-Color	10
	Cordial (H) w/o copy	Clear—Multi-Color	10
3 1/2 oz.	Boreal	Clear—Multi-Color	20
1996			
	Set of 3 1 1/2 oz. Shots	Black, Cobalt, Green—Gold (Green—Raised Decal)	35
1 1/2 oz.	Shot	Clear—Multi-Color	8
1 1/2 oz.	Shot	Black—Multi-Color	20
2 oz.	Whiskey Shot	Clear—Black/Gold	10
3 oz.	Jigger	Clear—Multi-Color	10
	Cordial w/copy	Clear—Multi-Color	15
	Cordial w/o copy	Clear—Multi-Color	10
	Cordial (H) w/copy	Clear—Multi-Color	10
	Cordial (H) w/o copy	Clear—Multi-Color	8
3 oz.	Boreal	Clear—Multi-Color	10

("Unauthorized" shots—all considered rare)

Year	Style	Color—Lettering	Value
1 1/2 oz.	Paneled Shot	Clear—Multi-Color	70
1 1/2 oz.	Paneled Shot	Clear—Etched	90

Year	Style	Color—Lettering	Value
1996 (continued)			
1 1/2 oz.	Shot	Cobalt—Multi-Color	100
1 1/2 oz.	Shot	Cobalt—Etched	80
1 1/2 oz.	Shot	Green—Multi-Color	85
1 1/2 oz.	Shot	Green—True Etched	100
1 1/2 oz.	Shot	Black—Etched	70
1 1/2 oz.	Shot	Clear—Etched	70
1 1/2 oz.	Shot	Wine—Multi-Color	sample
2 oz.	Flared Shooter	Clear—Multi-Color	60
2 oz.	Square Shot	Clear—Multi-Color	100
2 oz.	Square Shot	Clear—Etched	100
2 oz.	Ceramic (H)	White—Multi-Color	75
	Cordial (H) w/o copy	Clear—Etched	70
	Cordial w/o copy	Clear—Etched	70
3 oz.	Boreal	Clear—Etched	100
1997			
	Set of 3 1 1/2 oz. Shots	Wine, Green, Cobalt—Gold	40
1 1/2 oz.	Shot	Clear—Multi-Color	7
1 1/2 oz.	Shot	Clear—Black/Gold	8
1 1/2 oz.	Ceramic Shot	White—Graffiti	10
1 1/2 oz.	Ceramic Shot	White—Multi-Color	8
1 1/2 oz.	Shot	Black—Gold	7
1 1/2 oz.	Square Shot	Clear—Multi-Color	10
2 oz.	Whiskey Shot	Clear—Etched (Bacon's/McAlpin's)	50
2 oz.	Whiskey Shot	Clear—Gold	10
2 oz.	Cordial	Cobalt—Gold	9
3 oz.	Jigger	Clear—Gold	8
	Cordial w/o copy	Clear—Multi-Color	10
1998			
	Set of 3 1 1/2 oz. Shots	Green, Cobalt, Black—Gold	28
1 1/2 oz.	Shot	Black—Multi-Color	8
1 1/2 oz.	Ceramic Shot	White—Multi-Color	7
1 1/2 oz.	Shot	Clear—Multi-Color	7
1 1/2 oz.	Shot	Clear—Gold (Ltd. Edition, 1/1000) (Part of Triple Crown set)	30
2 oz.	Whiskey Shot	Clear—Etched (Bacon's/McAlpin's)	30
2 oz.	Whiskey Shot	Clear—Gold	8
2 oz.	Square Shot	Clear—Multi-Color	7
	Cordial w/o copy	Clear—Multi-Color	9
3 oz.	Jigger	Clear—Gold	8
	Lg. Shooter	Clear—Multi-Color	12
1999			
	Set of 3 1 1/2 oz. Shots	Green, Cobalt, Black—Gold	18
1 1/2 oz.	Stainless Steel Shot (Ltd. Edition, 1/1000)		16
1 1/2 oz.	Shot	Clear—Multi-Color	5
1 1/2 oz.	Shot	Clear—Checkerboard Wrap	7
2 oz.	Flared Shooter	Clear—Multi-Color	6
2 oz.	Whiskey Shot	Clear—Multi-Color	6
	Cordial w/o copy	Clear—Multi-Color	7
	Cordial (H) w/o copy	Clear—Multi-Color	7

Kentucky Derby Winners

The following is a list of the Kentucky Derby winners through 1998

Year	Winner
1998	Real Quiet
1997	Silver Charm
1996	Grindstone
1995	Thunder Gulch
1994	Go for Gin
1993	Sea Hero
1992	Lil E. Tee
1991	Strike the Gold
1990	Unbridled
1989	Sunday Silence
1988	#Winning Colors
1987	Alysheba
1986	Ferdinand
1985	Spend a Buck
1984	Swale
1983	Sunny's Halo
1982	Gato Del Sol
1981	Pleasant Colony
1980	#Genuine Risk
1979	Spectacular Bid
1978	**Affirmed**
1977	**Seattle Slew**
1976	Bold Forbes
1975	Foolish Pleasure
1974	Cannonade
1973	**Secretariat**
1972	Riva Ridge
1971	Canonero II
1970	Dust Commander
1969	Majestic Prince
1968	*Forward Pass
1967	Proud Clarion
1966	Kauai King
1965	Lucky Debonair
1964	Northern Dancer
1963	Chateaugay
1962	Decidedly
1961	Carry Back
1960	Venetian Way
1959	Tomy Lee
1958	Tim Tam
1957	Iron Liege
1956	Needles
1955	Swaps
1954	Determine
1953	Dark Star
1952	Hill Gail
1951	Count Turf
1950	Middleground
1949	Ponder
1948	**Citation**
1947	Jet Pilot
1946	**Assault**
1945	Hoop Jr.
1944	Pensive
1943	**Count Fleet**
1942	Shut Out
1941	**Whirlaway**
1940	Gallahadion
1939	Johnstown
1938	Lawrin
1937	**War Admiral**
1936	Bold Venture
1935	**Omaha**
1934	Cavalcade
1933	Brokers Tip
1932	Burgoo King
1931	Twenty Grand
1930	**Gallant Fox**
1929	Clyde Van Dusen
1928	Reigh Count
1927	Whiskery
1926	Bubbling Over
1925	Flying Ebony
1924	Black Gold
1923	Zev
1922	Morvich
1921	Behave Yourself
1920	Paul Jones
1919	**Sir Barton**
1918	Exterminator
1917	Omar Khayyam
1916	George Smith
1915	#Regret
1914	Old Rosebud
1913	Donerail
1912	Worth
1911	Meridian
1910	Donau
1909	Wintergreen
1908	Stone Street
1907	Pink Star
1906	Sir Huon
1905	Agile
1904	Elwood
1903	Judge Himes
1902	Alan-a-Dale
1901	His Eminence
1900	Lieut. Gibson
1899	Manuel
1898	Plaudit
1897	Typhoon II
1896	Ben Brush
1895	Halma
1894	Chant
1893	Lookout
1892	Azra
1891	Kingman
1890	Riley
1889	Spokane
1888	Macbeth II
1887	Montrose
1886	Ben Ali
1885	Joe Cotton
1884	Buchanan
1883	Leonatus
1882	Apollo
1881	Hindoo
1880	Fonso
1879	Lord Murphy
1878	Day Star
1877	Baden-Baden
1876	Vagrant
1875	Aristides

*Dancer's Image disqualified from first in 1968. Triple Crown winners in boldface. Race run at 1½ miles 1875-1895; 1¼ miles thereafter. #-a filly.

Acknowledgements

The editor would like to thank the following for their assistance in compiling The Blood-Horse Kentucky Derby Glasses Price Guide:

Joe Boone
John Clark
Cindy Pierson
Jim Powell
Vic Regnaud
Tom Sporney

Editor—Judy L. Marchman

Cover/Book Design—John D. Filer

Photography—Anne M. Eberhardt

Julep glasses and shot glasses courtesy of John Clark

1938 Julep Glass and Bakelites courtesy of Vic Regnaud

Photo of 1940 Dated Glass courtesy of Philip Musial